SHE MADE ME A POET

FOUND MYSELF A NEW ONE

PRATHUVEER SINGH

ISBN 979-888569038-6

Contents

Kandho ka bojh yhi rkh ke dekho apni mobobatt se mohobatt
nibhane ja ha hu mai

Kya wo surma lagati hogi ? kyuki mujhe toh aakhon se peene ka
shauk hai

, kya wo zulfen peeche htati hogi? kyuki Mujhe un zanzeeron mai
bandhne ka shauk hai

Kya wo Adaa dikhake ithlati hogi? Kyuki mujhe toh gurooriyat ka
shauk hai

Or kaaton ke khreeedar hai hum ,humee zindagi bhar zakham
mile hai

Kya wo gulabi itar lagati hogi ?

Kya wo gulabi itar lagati hogi ? kya wo bhi mujhe zehen mai utarti
hogi

Chalo sahab aaj vehem dur krte hai sare, us afreen se mulakaat
krne hum jare

Warna raat yehi sochte hogiii

Kya wo ye krti hogi kya wo ,wo krti hgi

DON'T BE SHY

THERE IS MOVEMENT IN LIFE WERE EACH ONE-OFF HAD OR GOING TO FEEL IN THE LIFE WHEN YOUR LOVE IS WITH YOU. THERE IS LITTLE SHYNESS IN THE ATMOSPHERE ONE OF THE LOVE BIRD IS GONNA SHY OR BLUSH WHOLE TIME OR UNTIL PERSON WAVE HAND TO SAY GOOD BY TO HER OR HIM. ONE PUT ON THE COURAGE TO EXPRESS THE FEELING TO HIS OR HER LOVE ONE.

Jo khena hai kehedo dekho sharmao nhi

Hath pakda hai humne palke uthalo dekho sharmao nhi

or jb tum dur se chalke aati ho toh lagta hai srume ka samandar tumhari aakhon mai duba hai

teri aaakhon ka surma mere hothon ki talash mai hai dekho sharmao nhi

sb karte honge tareef tere chehere ki are mai shayar hu mai aakhon se nasha karta hu

subh hoti hai meri teri muskan ke ujale se or surme ki chaav mai apni raat krta hu

hum tere 2 shabad bolne se pehele bhi irshaad bolne ko raazi hai zulfen peeche karli h toh kuch sunao zara sharmao nhi

kajal behenedo aaj aakhon se is khushi ko chupao nhi

Hath pakda hai humne palke uthalo dekho sharmao nhi..

THE BLESSED EYES

THERE IS THE TIME WE CAN ASSUME OR GUESS BY LOOKING INTO SOMEONES'S EYES ABOUT THERE FEELING. IF THE PERSON IS SAD, HAPPY, OR THERE IS SOMETHING WRONG WITH THE LIFE. WHEN YOU LOOK INTO YOUR LOVE ONE'S EYES THERE IS THE DIFFERENT THING YOU SEE IN IT. WHOLE WORLD LOOKS WASTE IN COMPARE TO HIS EYES JUST AND JUST YOU WANT TO LOOK INTO HER EYES. EYES ALSO EXPRESS FEELING. AFTER THAT ALL THING YOU HATE IN YOUR LIFE YOU START GETTING LOVE WITH EVERYONE UNTIL YOU HATED THEM ALL.

Hayee surme me bhigi hui aakhen uski

Kayi baar kamal hi kar deti h aakhen usi

Bhot koshish krta hu sb kuch yaad rakhu

Are sab kuch bhula hi deti h aakhen uski

Surma haseen hai ya aakhen uski

Shayar se uski bakiii sari shayariya cheen li

Bs uski aakhon pe likhta hu aaj kl kuch esa khel racha gyi ye aakhen uski

Or us aakhon mai amrit leke ghumti hai wo

Jise milgya fir wo aakhen uski

Or nazree milake rooh chuu deti hai yr

Use bilkul khabar nhi h kya kya kr gyi hai ye aakhen uski

Kya kya kr gyi h ye aakhen uski

FEVER

WHEN YOU STARTED LOVING SOMEONE. THAT
PERSON IMAGE GOES AROUND YOU UNTIL YOU STOP
LOVING OR STOP TALKING TO THAT PERSON.
PERSON ALWAYS WANT TO SEE THE FACE OF HIS/HER
SOULMATE AND THEN THEY FEEL THEMSELF FIT IN
THE WORLD. WORLD LOOKS LIKE DEAD PLANT
WHEN THEY CAN'T SEE THEM.

Aaaj kal mai chand ko mere chand ke chehre ki chandni ke baad
dekhta hu

Teri naarazgi ko meri naaarazgi se upper rakhne ke baad ,pyar se
tere chehere ke noor ko dekhne ke baad teri naarazgi dekhta hu

Or tujhe kya lagta hai is zindagi ke safar mai akela chord dunga
tujhe

Are mai toh subh uthte hi mere khayalo m tere khayalo se tere
chehere ki wo chamak ke baad asman dekhta hu

Or kya krna us chand ka jo feeka hai chandni mai

Mai toh meri chandni ke baad sara jahan dekhta hu

Are mai toh wo hu jo chand ko mere chand ki chandni ke baad
dekhta hu

FIRMLY LOVE

WHEN YOUR LOVE ONE BECOMES YOUR SAINT OR THE GOD. YOU WORSHIP YOUR LOVE MORE THEN ANYTHING IN THIS WORD. THE LIGHT OF YOUR LIFE BECOMES THE DESTROY OF YOUR DARKEST IN DREAM. THIS IS THE THING YOU STOP COMPLETING ABOUT YOUR LIFE.

Mai thaa udas kese apni akhon ko uski roshni se bharu

Mang rha tha rab se rastaa ke kese us se mulakaat kruu

Usi waqt usne mujhe aglee din hi mandir mai ro ba roo hone bulaa lia

Aee rab tune ye kesaa khel rachaa diaaa

Mai mushkil mai thaa ki sajdaaa kiskee samnee karuu

Aankh uthti toh chehera uska samnee thaa

Ishq khudaa se bdaa hota hai iskaa ek nateeja mere samnee tha

Mene usko manga mannat mai or usii ne hath pakad lia

Fir hona kya tha rab muskuraya humee dekh ke or sharma krr gulab ger diaa

Or fir tulsi hath mai dekar pyar ka prateek dia usne uske dil wale

mandir mai

Ek mulakaat esi bhi hui thi uske ghr ke paas wale mandir mai..

IT MAKES ME CRY

POET CONFESSES TO HIS LOVE THAT HE CAN'T SEE THE LIGHT OF HIS LIFE CRYING AROUND HIM. HE FEELS DESPAIR. THIS FIGHT BETWEEN THE POET AND HIS LOVE. POET THINKS HIMSELF THE CAUSE AND STARTER OF THE ARGUMENT. HER CASCADING DRIPS ARE CONVEYING A LOT OF INFORMATION OF HER PAIN. POET IS READY TO BATTLE WITH HER PAIN AND WANTS TO BRING HER JOYFUL GLORY FACE AROUND NATURE ONCE AGAIN.

Tri aakhen jab bhi roti hai

Mai kuch sehem sa jata hu

Jo kuch lafz rhe gye mujhme

Unme doshi sirf khud ko pata hu

Ek bade mehel si rani tu

Badi najuk si aadaye hai

Wo jo khwaishe hai aasman ki

Hath pakad tera hum hi chu aaye hai

Wo sharab ke pyali si mohobatt teri

Hum useee jam kr pee ayee hai

Wo hathh kaanp se jaate hai asuu bhee se jate hai

Jb pta chle apni mohobatt ki aakhon mai aasu aye hai

Mai sisak sa jata hu meri rahee jab bhi khoti hai

Pagal hu sahab pagal ho jata hu teri aaken jab bhi roti h

Mai nhi hu is zamane ka

Mujhe zeher bhi de tu dena

Wsee hoga ye rasamo ke khilaf

Magar kabar ko meri mitti bhi de toh tu dena

Ladegi jhukjaunga, hasegi khil sa jaunga

Yaad teri dikhegi andhere kamre yun raat bhar

Yaad meri hojayegi, mai tera ho sa jaunga

DROP OF MEMORIES

THE RAIN IS JOYFUL FOR SOME PEOPLE BUT SOME PEOPLE IN PAIN SAYS THAT "TODAY THE SKY IS CRYING IN THE PAIN." THIS IS WHERE POET COMPARE EACH PERSON FEELING WITH EACH DROP OF WATER FALLING FROM SKY WITH MEMORIES.

Chalte gye un bheegi raho pe

Barish barsi ya barsee aasu kuch pta nhi tha

Havaa chaliii mann garaj uthaa meraa

Andhi hava ki chali thi ya gum ki kuch pta ni tha

Rusvaa hua mausam bhi badal kale hokar aasu baras gye

Barsii yaad mere ghr hi ya uske ghr bhi barsaat hui kuch pta nhi tha

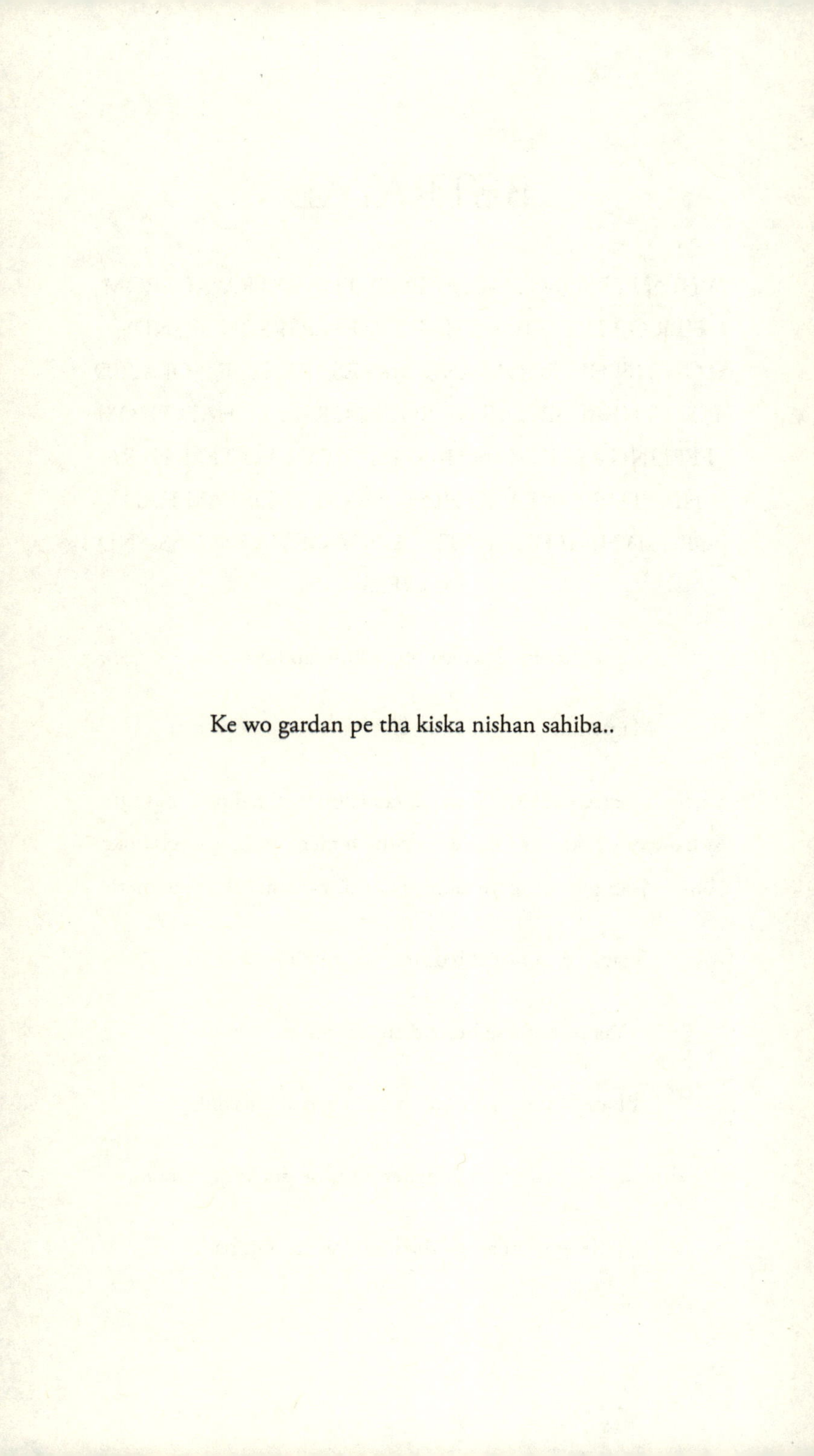

Ke wo gardan pe tha kiska nishan sahiba..

REALITY SMACKS YOUR HEAD

POET HAS CAME TO KNOW THE TRUTH AND THE REALITY OF LOVE IN THIS THE WORLD. HOW THE WORLD TREAT EACH OTHER? HOW A PERSON SHOWCASE IN FRONT HIMSELF TO OTHER BUT IN REALITY, PERSON HAS EAGER ENVIOUS FOR SOMEONE, AND DON'T CARE ABOUT FEELINGS.

Hai hakikat wohi jo bs mai likh rha hu

Baki sb jo likh rhe bs bhataka rhe us hakikat ko

Jo nikla zuban se wo toh mana fareb hai

Jo nikli kalam se ksee jhuthla skte hai us hakikat ko

Wo chand hakikat hai nhi

Wo daag hakikat hai uska

Ye ishq hakikat hai nhi

Wo drd hakikat hai uska

Ye nasha hakikat hai nhi

Wo mohobatt hakikat hai uska

Ye arzu hakikat hai nhi

Wo fehre hakikat hai uska

Ye aakhne jhapakti hai nhi

Tera chehera hakikat hai uska

Ye mann samjhta hi nhi

Wo jana hai hakikat h uska

Ye sham hakikat hai nhi

Dekha or paya latakti lash hakikat hai sbka..

WHEN I WRITE

POET WAS TRYING TO ADDRESS THE FEELING WHEN
HE WRITES A POEM TOO MANY THOUGHTS TOO
MANY QUESTIONS CAME IN HIS MIND? MEMORIES
WEREN'T HELPING DOWN ON PAPER. JOLTING
MEMORIES HAD SHUTTERED HIM.

Kalam chalne lagi toh aasu baras gye mere

Fir Tasveer dekhi uski toh savalon pe saval uthgye mere

Gilii aakhen leke chal pda mai zeher peene

Mekhane mai dekh log bole aagya shayar aasu ke sath sharab
peene

Dekh saki (the girl who pore your glass of liquor in bar) ne uski
tasveer mangli

Ke kese ye aasu saj gye

Fir dekh tasveer muskurakar boli khushnaseeb ho janab jo husan
ke hatoh se zinda bach gye

Or Kyu hai chup kyu drd ko seeta h

Yha sb drd leke ek dusre se yehi puchte hai ,ki kon hai wo jo aasu
ke sath sharab peeta h?

WHO IS A POET?

IN THIS, THE POET IS TRYING TO CONNECT NORMAL PEOPLE AND A POET WITH HASHISH DRUG AND CHARAS DRUG AS IT IS SAID THAT LIVING LIFE IS DIFFICULT BUT DYING IS NOT AS SAME AS THAT HASHISH IS MADE BY GRINDING DEAD PLANTS OF CANNABIS AS NORMAL PEOPLE DOES'NT HAVE ANY HURDLE ON THEIR LIFE AND CHARAS IS MADE UP OF GRINDING LIVING PLANTS OF CANNABIS AS POET HAD MANY SCRATCHES IN THEIR LIFE THAT'S WHY THEY ARE POET.

Ek andheri raat m chain se bethke bhi bechan ishq hai wo shayar

Tuttee dil kaa or bigdtee leheje kaa woo nuskh hai wo shayar

Kee bheegi aakhon seee bhi naa royee or lahu luhan hoke bhi na mare wo jism hai wo shayar

Mohobatt , aree nadaniii hi khelooo

Magar is khel ki girfat mai hai wo shayar

Or Hashish sa hai insan marne ke baad peesa gya, jee te jii peesa gya nasha charas h wo shayar

Orr kareeeb naa aao barbad hone ka khtraa haii

FLAWS

AT TIME DEAD END. ROAD GAVE THE CHANCE TO STOP BUT THE DRIVER PASSENGER MISS OUT IT. FURY WORD JUMBLE DOWN, THE ONE IS RIGHT BUT OTHER ONE IS WRONG.

Mere hisab se ye chand hai

Tere hisab ek putla daag ka

Mere hisab se hai ye hava nashili si

Tere hisab se saanp ek zeherila sa

Tu mane ek raah ko apni zindagi

Mai manu har raah ko apni zindagi

Teriii raah akasar suuni hoti h

Meri har rhaa tujhpe ake khatam hoti h

Ye taare dikhte mujhe jugnoo se

Tujheee lagte aasman mai daag

Tere haath m tha rakeeb ka hath

Mere galeee mai latk rhi tere ishq ki raag

Tu pari hai farishta hai

Mai toh aadha pagal hu

Tere hisaab se toh tu aasman hai

Toh bta mai tere kis aasman ka badal hu

ALLEGATION

WHEN PEOPLE POINTS OUT ON POET THAT THE WORD POET WROTE ARE JUST IMAGINARY AND THIS MUCH OF PAIN NONE CAN TOLERATE. THE POET REPLIED:

Seedha ladkaa bikhar gya usdin

Fir wo panno par itihas bnane chala tha

Uthi ugliaa ishq bayan krne par uske , magar sir drd se jhuk gye

Akhon m nami lekar jb pda ke wo ishq ki kayenaat likh gya tha

Or zindagi toh khud bewafa hai , hum toh fir bhi piyadee hai uske

Bewafaon ke haq m kuch wo esa likh gya tha

Uske shabad ko yaad kia jayega aasuon se

Or har shabd par aasuon ke janaze niklenge

Pta chlega jb kisi se ishq bhi wo kiti mohobat se kar gyaa tha

Or jaam ,saharab ,shabab shauk nhi the uskee

Mekhaane mai beth ek aashiq apni majboori likh gya tha

Or ek ehesan krr mujhpee itnaa sach naa bol

Jaam lete lete shayar ye puri gazal kaat gya thai

ACCEPTED

WHEN BOY ASK A GIRL FOR SOMETHING. ANYTHING GIRL REPLY IS ALWAYS ACCEPTED BY THE BOY WITHOUT A QUESTION. THAT'S WHO BOYS ARE MAD IN LOVE.

Paas aake muskuratee toh zyada aacha rheta

Dur rhekar hi sharmana hai toh bhi thiek hai

Agar haathon se pilate toh zyada bdiaa rheta

Agar aakhon se peelana hai toh bhi thiek h

Agar kuch gazale sunate toh zyada aacha rheta

Kangan hi chankane hai toh bhi thk hai

Avaz dekar bulate toh jyada aacha rheta

Nazre hi jhukani hai toh bhi thk hai

Isharo mai chhat pe bulate toh zyada aacha rheta

Chhat par rhekar muskana hai toh bhi thk h

Izhaar krke jatate toh aacha rheta

DON'T WASTE YOUR LIFE

NO MORE, SORRY, WE ARE DONE HERE, WE CAN'T GO FURTHER, I AM NOT HAPPY WITH YOU AND MORE WORD TO ADDED BY THE PERSON WHO KEEPS THE APPLEALING OF THE BREAK UP , THIS ARE WORLD ARE GONNA COME IN YOUR LIFE NOT TODAY OR IT MIGHT BE TOMRROW. IF YOU REACH THE MARRIAGE WITH SOULMATE THEN YOU MUST GOOD THINGS IN PAST LIFE. BUT VERY ANNOYING IS THE BREAK UP WHERE YOU DON'T WHY THIS HAPPEN.

kisi haseena ke peche apni zindagi kharab mat kr

Dekh mat kr

Ye sapne jo adhure maa baaap ki akhon m asu ban latak rhe

Us aasun m bhi hr ek zakham par namak hai

Or usi haseena ke ashiq har ghr m latak rhe

Or tere har ek aasu pr bhi uski aakhon mai chamak hai

Dekh mat kr

Mat kr ye ishq mohobatt ke vaade

Jo kbhi nhi pure ho pate

Rhe jatee sirf bewafai ke chate

Dimag rota, na hum sun pate

Ki hum kash uski sun paate

Or woo nashila padarth rkhtiii haii

Use kyiii nashemann panah denge

Tere ps kurbani ko kuch nhi isliye log tujhe sirf salah denge

Dekh mat kr

kisi haseena ke peche apni zindagi kharab mat kar..